CW00797075

1. Wise Men Three
2. Cherished
3. Are You Ready
4. Radiant Glory
5. Yield
6. The Shadow of Doubt
7. A Widow's Miracle
8. Without a Doubt
9. Thank Goodness
10. Forgiveness
11. Blessing at Bethesda
12. Answer Me
13. Final Passage
14. Holy is the Lamb   -   Earth Angels
15. The Chosen - In Seven Days God Created Man
16. The Gift
17. The Apple, Grape and Olive
18. Hope for Tomorrow
19. Fili Mi   (My Son)
20. The Visit
21. No Doubt   -   Passer-by
22. Look Up

Wise Men Three

From the east the magi came
On donkey, ass and camel train,
Following a heavenly star,
They travelled on from lands afar.
At Herod's bidding they were sent
To find a babe his foul intent;
Across the dunes the travellers rode,
Each carrying a precious load
Of treasures for the new born King.
A Saviour Child, now born, would bring
Peace on Earth, goodwill to men,
Three Wise Men rode to Bethlehem,
There they knelt and homage paid
Amongst the ox and ass a babe,
By a manger cold and bare
Is where they laid their gifts most rare
To this Holy Child and Heavenly King.
An innocent, vulnerable tiny thing
A dream had warned them not to stay
But to journey home a different way.

Cherished

God blessed a humble maiden in Nazareth long ago
He favoured her to bare his Son and raise him as her own
Her soul was pure her heart was true, her purpose was quite clear
The Mother of Salvation, revered throughout the years

Now mothers are a special breed their love is quite unique
Sincere and unconditional and with their heart they speak
They hold us when we're poorly and wipe away our tears
Listen to our worries and banish all our fears.

They walk this life beside us and take us by the hand
Teach us all we need to know 'til strong and tall we stand
They're always there to lend a hand, encourage and support,
To guide us when we're troubled and cry when we're distraught

There's nothing that they wouldn't do to keep us safe from harm
Their love's forever with us no matter where we roam.
God gave us each an angel to cherish as our own
To spend a lifetime with us and named this angel mum.

God bless these special ladies, they're from a heavenly mould
Their smiles are full of sunshine and their hearts are made of gold
There's a rainbow linking every wish as they sweep across the nations
Our mothers are our life blood for they are of God's creation.

Are You Ready?

Are you ready for Christ when he comes?
Are you sure that you won't be the one?
To be caught unawares as our Saviour prepares
For there won't be a fanfare or drums

He'll come in the still of the night
Unexpected yet still in plain sight
Are you ready for him - will you welcome him in?
And be happy to stand in his light.

He will come not to rule but to serve,
Stay alert and be sure to observe
All the signs that he sends, all the signals and trends
For your vision, should never be blurred

Are you ready to look in his face?
Feel the wonder and power of his grace
Can you love as he taught and forgive as you ought?
Are you ready for heavens embrace?

Radiant Glory

The Son of God took mortal form in Bethlehem one night,
He left his safe celestial home to put our world to rights
As babe, as child, as adult too He lived God's holy plan
A teacher who could heal the lame - He still was just a man.

He preached his father's message - forgiveness, peace and love
That some indeed would live to see the day God's kingdom come.
With Peter, James and John they say, He climbed a mountain high
To take some time, to be alone, to pray beneath the sky.

Disciples sat in wonder as their Master went to speak
To Moses and Elijah upon that mountain peak,
A shining light encased them, so pure and full of grace,
Then all at once the watchers saw - A change came on his face.

A voice was heard quite clearly – 'Here's my beloved Son,
To him you each must listen, I'm so pleased with all he's done'
Jesus leant and touched them – 'get up, don't be afraid'
Their Master stood before them, the light had turned to shade.

'Tell no-one of this vision, of what happened in this place
Until the day the Son of Man has risen from the grave.'

Yield

It's not a rite of passage, the good seed on the land,
We shouldn't take for granted the food that's in our hands.

We never can be certain that a harvest will succeed,
Or that as the seasons alter we'll have all the food we need.

We can calculate and quantify, we can strategize and plan
Breed new strains of crops and grain to yield the most they can.

Advances in technology should make each harvest bigger
But we have never had control of what our Lord delivers

Patiently we tend the land the only way we can.
But in the end we wait and yield to God's Almighty plan.

All we can do is scatter the good seed on the land,
Then, when the planting's over, the rest is in God's hands.

The Shadow of Doubt

Didymus, one of the twelve, and Lord's disciple you could tell,
He wasn't' there when next Christ stood amongst his chosen
brotherhood,
Who eagerly with one accord, informed him they'd seen the Lord!

But doubting Thomas was unsure, how could this be, Christ was no more
He died upon that awful cross, nailed and speared his life was lost.
They stood and watched him die that day and yet he clearly heard them
say
That they had plainly seen the Lord, he longed for more than just their
word.

A week passed by and Thomas tried, in disbelief he did reside
Doubts were high and faith was weak, the future seemed so very bleak
Could not believe his friends reports, he needed more, he needed hope,
He yearned for God to intervene and show him what his friends had seen.

'I won't believe until I see the wounds upon his hands and feet,
Touch the gash within his side, then I'll know my Lord's alive'
So at a meeting of the twelve, behind locked doors so all was well
Christ did manifest that day, and Thomas saw and touched and prayed.

'Today you've touched my hands and side, and seen me with your own two
eyes
So stop the doubting and believe, have faith and all will be revealed'
'My Lord, my God', his soft reply, his heart was full, his tears were dry,
Now you have seen and know the truth, how blessed are those who need
no proof,
It is for them the angels sing, they'll know the grace true faith will bring.

A Widow's Miracle

Travelling to town with Jesus, on his right and left
Met some mourners on the way, carrying their dead.

The body of a mother's son upon a bier was laid
A tragic vision to behold amongst that grim parade

The plight of that poor widow was a wretched sight to see,
Observing her the Lord was moved and went to intercede.

'Don't cry' he softly said to her, then turned towards the youth,
'Young man, I say to you Get Up', the crowd were so confused.

The boy arose from off the bier, perplexed yet quite alive
And sat there talking to the Lord, that stranger by his side

Who gently ushered this sweet this lad back towards his mum
As she gazed in awe and wonderment at what the Lord had done

They had a prophet in their midst, a messenger from God
Sent down to help them understand the power of Peace and Love

A miracle that day was seen in that little town
And news of what had happened there soon spread throughout the land.

Without a Doubt

The faith of a child is a wondrous thing
Knows nothing of doubt or of fear
So close to God when they enter this realm
Still at peace and their trust is sincere

Doubting is normal, it's just what we do
we always need proof to believe
Ask so many questions we get quite confused
then can't see the wood for the trees

Now the faith of our little ones, so meek and mild
Is laid bare in their very first years
Their innocent trust can be tarnished and torn
By wisdom, by reason and fear

Faith is a word that is bandied about
Such a scary, untenable state
But we all live in faith every day of the year
To think that we don'ts a mistake

We have faith that each morning we'll wake from our sleep
And trust that we'll take our next breath,
That tomorrow will come and the world will still turn
And our heart will still beat in our breast

Just one step further to have faith in our God
We're all his children you see
There's so much hope in the eyes of a child
They're our future and their faith is the key.

Thank Goodness

Did you say hello this morning to your family or a friend,
Seek advice, need some help, perhaps have some to lend?
Pop in for a coffee, a gossip or a chat.
Comment on the weather, moan at this or that?
Did you natter on the telephone before you left for church?
Thanking friends for being there when life seemed at its worst.
A problem shared, a problem halved, we know this to be true
How many conversations did he have this day with you?
When you arose this morning did you say 'good morning Lord?
Take a moment over breakfast to just stop and have a word.
Did you recognise his voice and then share your points of view?
Thank him just for being there to help to guide you through.
Take some time to listen, to contemplate and mend,
Trusting that upon his love you know you can depend.
Better than the best of friends he's always on your side,
Wanting you to talk to him and waiting to reply.
Explain to him your feelings, even have a laugh,
Sometimes life is funny, events can seem so daft.
Say your piece, don't be shy, let him know in future,
Life isn't always serious; he has a sense of humour.
Like any real relationship it never is plain sailing,
You will get cross or disagree when you feel that life is failing,
It's very easy to forget that although at times life's hard,
Man can do his worst but thank goodness God's in charge.

Forgiveness

Forgiveness takes such strength of the heart
To bare no malice, take no part
In vengeance whispered by the soul,
So clean the slate, just let it go
Absolve the hurt that's caused by man,
Just turn your cheek, through love you can
When you're bruised, and feeling small
Then bow your head, he'll hear you call,
His love will draw you close to him
And guide you gently from within.

It isn't right for you or me
To ask the Lord to intercede
If we are simply unprepared
And can't forgive, it isn't fair
To daily ask, in silent prayer,
'Forgive me Lord, for I have erred'
Don't let your heart be vexed and sore
Forgive yourself and know for sure
That daily he forgives our faults,
So pay it forward as we're taught

Life is cruel and words are tough,
Mistakes are made, by them and us,
When you hurt from wounded pride,
Let mercy heal you deep inside;
For life's too short to hold a grudge
So live in peace and light and love.
Our Father told us what to do,
Love yourself - and others too.
But when we falter, and we do,
The strength of Christ will pull us through.

Blessing at Bethesda

Could you feel what he felt as he lay on the ground
So helpless, so hopeless and sad
No one came forward to lend him a hand
Or ask what was wrong with this man.
He knew that no way could he enter the pool
As he lay all alone on the sand
Yet, he was still there with no reason to hope
And no clue what the future had planned.

So loud the commotion from inside the crowd
Could it really be heading his way?
Should he be scared of the voice overhead
Surely what was it going to say
What do you need, do you want to be healed?
Was the question that came from above
38 years I have waited and hoped
Someday I'd be cared for and loved

Arise old man, take your bed and walk
You'll not be needing the pool.
Then the limbs which for years had laid dead by his side
Sprang to life and then started to move
Leaders loudly declared this should never have been
It defiled the Sabbath you see
But the man took himself to the temple and prayed
Giving thanks, he was healed, he was free.

Answer Me

Your answer is before you as a whisper on the wind,
If only you could hear it t'would make your spirit sing,
You won't receive a letter or a parcel in the post,
Or a verification email 'regards the Holy Ghost',
There is no bolt of lightning, no signpost in the sky,
We never will be there to kneel before the holy child.
The miracles we witness are around us every day,
We take them all for granted as we scurry on our way;
We miss the signs he sends us, we think that we know best,
Upon our simple knowledge, our faith now clearly rests.
We assimilate his message the only way we can,
We use the tools provided, the childlike mind of man.
It's no wonder that in all of this so many get confused,
Our faith is two dimensional, the third we cannot view.
When lost, alone and stranded is where you stand in life,
Waiting for a signal, where doubt is truly rife,
Look at natures marvels, let them fill your breast,
Open wide your senses, allow them to ingest
Life's wonders all around you, phenomenon unique,
It's here that you will start to find the answers that you seek.
When next you hear the wind as it whistles down the lane,
Close your eyes and listen he might just call your name.

Final Passage

Did you ever notice his memories would change?
Understand the reason,
Or think that it was strange?
Did you look and see the changes on his face,
Watch his frame diminish?
Or deny that it's the case?
Don't take away his dignity.
Don't take away his pride,
Don't show him all the pity
You hold there locked inside.
Allow him now to pass in peace,
Let his spirit soar;
Be present at the moment
God opens up his door.
Remember all the good times,
Keep them safe within,
Just be still and wonder
How tomorrow should begin.
Grant yourself permission,
Allow your tears to flow.
Accept that in a little while
Everyone will know
That another of God's children
Has found his way back home.

Holy is The Lamb

Born the holy Lamb of God,
A precious gift from God above,
Born to change the path of man,
To instigate God's holy plan
Born into a world of sin,
To save mankind from deep within,
Born to die that we might live,
This Holy Lamb his life did give.
Holy is the Lamb of God,
Our Lord and Master, King of love.

Earth Angels

Earth angels live among us, hiding in plain sight,
Helping when they're needed plus doing what is right,
They're always there to lend a hand when life has been so cruel,
They pick us up and brush us off and gently help us through.

Then just as fast they're gone again, their impact has been felt,
We cannot know the form they'll take or recognise their face,
And yet we feel the help they bring, and the difference that they make.

At will we cannot find them, no matter what your view,
When you really need them, they will come to you.

Chosen

Chosen to laugh - chosen to cry,
Chosen to love or chosen to sigh.
Chosen to give - chosen to try,
Chosen to live yet chosen to die.
Chosen to heal - chosen to mend,
Chosen to teach then chosen to tend.
Chosen to shine and chosen to guide,
Chosen to save not chosen to hide.
Chosen to listen and to obey
The Father's will, without being afraid.
Chosen to watch, chosen to be
Betrayed by a kiss, for you and for me.
Chosen to suffer then to ascend,
Chosen my Saviour, Redeemer and Friend.

In Seven Days God Created Man

God created earth and earth gave birth to man
Evolution, after all, was guided by his hand.
1. Firstly came the great Big Bang, the day the universe began,
2. Releasing gases near and far, condensing neatly into stars,
3. From shining stars so very hot came forth our mortal melting pot.
4. Swirling massive clouds of might new solar systems put to flight;
5. On rocks the mighty seas were formed from whence organic life was born,
6. A basis for all life on earth, this melting pot did then give birth
7. Such simple cells soon split and grew, new species oozed from cosmic goo,
In seven ways God created man, Evolution was His plan.

The Gift

Five thousand strong they came to be
Beside the Sea of Galilee
To watch the healing of the sick,
Where miracles were not a trick,
As Jesus gently laid his hands
On every woman, child and man,
This noisy crowd would soon need fed,
A little boy gave all he had -

Five loaves, two fishes were his gift,
To help was all this young lad wished,
So Jesus took the precious food,
Gave thanks and shared it with the crowd,
Changed their water into wine,
That day their banquet was divine,
Revealed – no longer just a man,
Disciples scared what was his plan?

That crowd they ate without a care,
Left overs gathered, lots to spare,
12 baskets for another time,
Nothing wasted, all was fine,
Then Jesus made it very clear,
The food of God won't disappear,
All he wants for us to do
Is trust in him and his Son too.

Jesus said in solemn truth
It was not Moses who fed you,
Heaven and earth hand in hand
Together fed the soul of man,
The Light of Christ shines pure and bright;
He truly is the bread of life.

The Apple, Grape and Olive

The apple, grape and olive
The corn and wheat and tare
Are provided by our Father
For all mankind to share;
In order to sustain us
Each day throughout the year
These blessings are our lifeline
That we trust will just appear
So think for just one moment
Of these gifts that he supplies
As this food that feeds his children
Is his manna from on high.
He sends to us the sun and rain
The wind to spread the seed
And nurtures all things growing
So our harvest will succeed
The apple, grape and olive,
The corn, the wheat, the tare
Are examples of God's bounty
Produced for all to share.
So say thank you to our Father
Holy Spirit from on high
We must never take for granted
All the fruits this earth supplies.

Hope for Tomorrow

Daddy, why are you wearing a poppy?
And what is it trying to say?
Why is this act of remembering?
So special on only one day?

Mummy, why are you buying a poppy?
And why does it have to be red?
Why just the blood not the body
Is all we recall of the dead?

Granny, why do all of the poppies,
Worn by the thousands today,
Fall out of favour tomorrow,
Then just get thrown away?

Granddad, why does the heart of the poppy
Look like a black lump of coal?
All those soldiers that died for our freedom,
Surely they had hearts made of gold.

Daddy please can I wear a poppy,
But I want mine to be white,
I want to hope for the future,
That next time we might get it right!

Fili Mi
(My Son)

Imagine your son,
Imagine his cry.
Imagine how you would feel watching him die,
Hung on that cross, lost and alone,
Ripping your heart out with each piercing moan,
Unable to help
Unable to try
Unable to understand, screaming out 'Why?
What has he done, why can't you see,
Get him down, set him free, crucify me!'

Imagine the tears of his Father above
His beloved Son died
Asking where he had gone.
Imagine his fury,
Imagine his wrath,
Salvation of mankind, look what it had cost.
Now paid in full with that last dreadful cry,
Forgiveness not vengeance his only reply.
We cannot conceive what transpired on that hill
We may spend our life trying, but we never will.

The Visit

The world and his wife are coming to tea,
The world and his wife plus one,
There's Jacob and Mary, there's Peter and John,
There's Matthew and there's Paul.

The world and his wife are coming for tea,
The world and his wife that's all.
With Andrew, Thomas and Philip as well
It's Thomas however that you must all tell
Of what has befallen the great and the good
Of how he has risen and in front of you stood,

The world and his wife are coming to tea,
The world and his wife are here,
Break out the bread, the fish and the mead,
Hand them out slowly and see them exceed
All expectations from the first to the last,
No one left hungry, all portions surpassed

The world and his wife came over for tea,
The world and his wife were here,
Their visit was special, above and beyond,
They weren't all sat chatting, no very far from,
They witnessed in wonder the events of the day,
Then all left in awe with nothing to say.

No Doubt

Can I not rely on you?
Are you not my friend?
Are you not the one on whom
I know I can depend?
The master of my demons,
And shepherd of my woes,
The shining light within my heart
That everyone can know.

I'm sure I can rely on you,
My Saviour and my friend,
You died for my salvation,
A grim and tragic end.
You lived your life a teacher
Of peace and love and faith,
A perfect pure example
To the shameful human race.

Passer-by

Is life really worth so little, does the passer-by not see
That the plight of man is intertwined with the life of you and me.

With the homeless in the city, with the helpless left at home,
And each and every traveller no matter where they roam.

Be kind to one another, take care lest it might be
You that's in the gutter, pray your passer-by won't leave.

Look Up

See a twinkle in the sky,
Just like the blinking of God's eye
And in that moment, we feel safe,
For its then we've glimpsed his face.

Felt his breath on every breeze,
Gently whisper through the trees
As the Universe extends,
Our Faith in God should never end.

Through every trouble, test and trial,
His love will guide us all the while,
Share our woes and hear our prayers,
Deep inside we'll feel him there.

I may not choose my path in life
But by God I know it's right
My hearts at peace, my soul is calm,
All hope restored and fear disarmed.

Without our faith, we're lost and small,
So vulnerable, adrift, alone
Confused we stumble and we roam,
It's only Faith can lead us home.

18988080R00016

Printed in Great Britain
by Amazon